ENGLAND
UNDER THE
STUARTS

COLLECTIONS IN THE ASHMOLEAN MUSEUM
FROM JAMES I TO QUEEN ANNE

MOIRA HOOK
ARTHUR MACGREGOR

GW00482190

ASHMOLEAN MUSEUM . OXFORD
2003

ASHMOLEAN MUSEUM PUBLICATIONS

ARCHAEOLOGY, HISTORY AND CLASSICAL STUDIES

ANCIENT EGYPTIAN AND NEAR EASTERN CIVILIZATIONS
Ancient Egypt
Ancient Near East

MINOAN CRETE
Arthur Evans and the Palace of Minos
Arthur Evans, Knossos and the Priest King
Before Knossos: Arthur Evans's Travels in the Balkans and Crete
Arthur Evans's Travels in Crete 1894–1899

GREEK AND ROMAN LIFE
Ancient Greek Terracottas
The Ancient Romans
Sporting Success in the Greek and Roman World
Eat, Drink and be Merry – the food and drink of
the Ancient Greeks and Romans

BRITISH SOCIAL AND ECONOMIC HISTORY
Life and Death in the Iron Age
Medieval England
Tudor England
Pots and People

Moira Hook and Arthur MacGregor have asserted the moral right to be identified as the authors of this work

ISBN 1 85444 179 5

British Library Cataloguing-in-publication Data
A catalogue record for this publication is available from the British Library

Front cover: Thomas Toft charger fig.47
Back cover: Salver made from the Boscobel Oak

Publishing Consultant – Ian Charlton
Typeset in Janson and designed by Geoff Green
Printed and bound in Singapore by Craft Print International, 2002

UNIVERSITY OF OXFORD
ASHMOLEAN MUSEUM

Contents

Bibliography

The Arundel Collection (Apollo 144 (1996) no 413).

J. Ayers, O. Impey & J. V. G. Mallet, 1900 *Porcelain for Palaces,* exh. cat., British Museum (London).

D. D. Boyden, 1969. *The Hill Collection of Musical Instruments in the Ashmolean Museum, Oxford* (Oxford).

A. Fraser 1973. *Cromwell* (London).

A. Fraser, 1996. *The Gunpowder Plot.* (London).

R. & T. Kelly, 1987. *A City at War: Oxford 1642–46* (Cheltenham).

A. MacGregor (ed.), 1983. *Tradescant's Rarities* (Oxford).

J. MacKay, 1984. *A History of Modern English Coinage* (London & New York).

F. MacLean, 1970. *A Concise History of Scotland* (London).

M. Newby, 2000. *Glass of Four Millennia* (Oxford).

T. Schroder, 1988. *English Domestic Silver 1500–1900* (London).

G. M. Trevelyan, 1946 *England under the Stuarts* (London).

R. Walker, 1997. *Miniatures (A selection of miniatures in the Ashmolean Museum)* (Oxford).

Acknowledgements

The authors are grateful to Richard Sharp for constructive criticism of the text while in typescript. Figs. 38, 45, 46 and 55 are reproduced by courtesy of PotWeb, the Ashmolean's on-line ceramics project: for further details visit www.PotWeb.org

Fig. 28 is reproduced by courtesy of Mr Roger Lushington, whose family has owned the tankard illustrated since 1699.

Key to Illustrations

England under the Stuarts

T HE STEWARTS were hereditary kings of Scotland from the time of Robert the Bruce, whose forebears had been stewards in service of the king since the twelfth century. The spelling changed to Stuart when the young Queen Mary, daughter of James V and Mary of Guise, used the Anglo-French style of her surname; the same spelling was used by Lord Darnley, her husband and the father of James VI.

James Stuart (1566–1625), King of Scotland, succeeded to the throne of England on the death of Queen Elizabeth I in 1603. As the great-great-grandson of Henry VII, whose daughter Margaret had married James IV of Scotland, James's claim to the English throne was well founded. His mother Mary Queen of Scots had abdicated and

1. Medal of James I, struck 1624. The King wears a fashionable hat fastened with a jewel; at his neck is a George of the Order of the Garter. The legend proclaims his dominion over 'Great Britain', France and Ireland'.

2. James I's Great Seal. The arms of the Tudors are quartered with the lion rampant of Scotland; the Irish harp also appears for the first time in the third quarter. This wax seal shows the form used in Scotland, with the Scottish arms given precedence.

3. Watch *c.* 1610, engraved with the Stuart arms and initials of Henry, Prince of Wales. The Scotsman David Ramsay, who became Royal Clockmaker to James I in 1613, made three watches for Prince Henry; this may be one of them.

fled from Scotland in 1567 and, after twenty years of exile, was executed in 1587 by decree of Queen Elizabeth, leaving her infant son to inherit the kingdom. So it was as an experienced monarch aged thirty-seven years, married to Anne of Denmark and with a young family, that James VI of Scotland rode south to claim the throne as James I of England – the first king to reign over two countries that had been habitual enemies through many centuries. Nevertheless, his English subjects warmly welcomed him, perhaps optimistic that the stability and success that Scotland had enjoyed during his reign might be repeated; their enthusiasm, however, owed more to thankfulness for a peaceful succession than to his personal popularity. Aware that he had been educated by eminent scholars and that he had a reputation for some political skill, the English had high hopes of their new king (though they were taken aback by his rough manners and slovenly appearance). Within eighteen months James had

announced that the united kingdoms of England and Scotland would now be known as Great Britain, though it would be nearly a century before the term gained the force of law.

Early optimism was soon deflated as James's reign proved to be troubled. On the death in 1612 of Robert Cecil, the great Secretary of State whom James had inherited from Elizabeth, he chose advisers from favourites and men of dubious worth. He also attracted the outrage of some elements of Parliament by his attachment to the doctrine of the Divine Right of Kings, maintaining that the monarch derived his authority from God and could not be held to account by earthly authority. James's inconsistency in his dealings with Papists and Puritans offended both communities: when Catholic sympathizers attempted to blow up the Houses of Parliament a wave of anti-Catholic feeling swept the country; Nonconformists were also persecuted at this time and Puritans, resentful of James's policies, set sail for America in some numbers. For all that, some benefits arose under James: peace was negotiated with Spain and war was avoided for his entire reign; he established a lasting union between England and Scotland and when, in 1611, the Authorized Version of the Bible was published, a lasting treasure was bequeathed to the nation.

When James died, unlamented, it was a younger son – not for the first time in English history – who inherited the throne, owing to the early death in 1612 of Henry, Prince of Wales. Charles I (reigned 1625–49) may have been possessed of more attractive qualities than his father, but had inherited both his belief in the Divine Right and notably poor judgement in his choice of advisers. Less approachable than James, aloof and inordinately stubborn, Charles was reluctant to allow his actions to be guided by any of his counsellors and in 1629 he renounced the services of his government, ruling in person for the next eleven years. In an attempt to raise funds Charles eventually recalled Parliament in 1640, but in a climate of factionalism and mistrust the nation disintegrated into Civil War, with the populace split between the causes of King and Parliament. (Even within Parliament itself there was a range of opinion, in which the Royalist members found themselves increasingly alienated as opinions

4. Charles I, copy after Antonie van Dyck. Charles I was an ambitious patron of the arts, commissioning Van Dyck to paint his courtiers and Rubens to decorate the ceiling of the Banqueting House in Whitehall. He accumulated one of the greatest art collections of Europe, which was sold off by Parliament under the Commonwealth.

5. Bust of Oliver Cromwell, by Joseph Nollekens. Worked in Carrara marble and standing some 60cm high, this is a forceful image of a bareheaded Cromwell in armour. Since Nollekens lived a century after Cromwell, the likeness evidently was not been created at first hand.

6. Charles II, by John Riley. The middle-aged King is shown in armour with a lace cravat and wearing the blue sash of the Order of the Garter. As a boy of twelve Charles had been at his father's side at the Battle of Edgehill.

7. Coronation medal of Queen Anne, 1702. Anne, brought up as a Protestant at the insistence of her uncle Charles II, married Prince George of Denmark and supported the cause of William III and her elder sister Mary against James II.

polarized). Hostilities broke out in 1642 and the beginning of the end was signalled by the execution of the King in 1649 and the declaration of a republic, to be known as the Commonwealth.

The Parliamentary forces in the Civil War had been led latterly by Oliver Cromwell, who was installed as Lord Protector of England from 1651 until his death seven years later. Cromwell was a Member of Parliament when the troubles began and was entirely without military experience; nevertheless, he became a brilliant strategist and commander. The exercise of rule in a virtual dictatorship was not what he had intended, but Cromwell found it impossible to unite all sides in Parliament and his attempt to secure unity through the imposition of military rule heralded a notably joyless period for the people of England. The last vestiges of opposition within Parliament evaporated on 6 December 1648 when 'Pride's Purge' resulted in the arrest of forty-five Members and the exclusion of a further 186. When Cromwell died in 1658 and the country faced the prospect of rule by his ineffectual son Richard, the military leaders (notably General

Monck) decided further disunity could best be avoided by the restoration of the monarchy.

In May 1660 Charles II returned to London from exile in The Netherlands, to an enthusiastic reception from an optimistic populace. Charles had been proclaimed King by the Scots after his father's execution in 1649 and, with their support, Charles had continued to fight against Cromwell until his final defeat at Worcester in 1651. Following his escape from the battlefield he spent six weeks as a fugitive, during which time the famous incident of his evasion of capture by hiding in an oak tree at Boscobel House took place (see back cover); thereafter he made good his escape to the Continent, where he was to spend the following nine years in exile.

Charles II is popularly remembered for the pleasures he took from life but his reign saw the successful restoration of constitutional government and he played an important personal role in the founding of enlightened institutions such as the Royal Society and in the patronage of figures such as Sir Christopher Wren, who was to play such a crucial role in the aftermath of the Great Fire of London in 1666. At his death in 1685, Charles left the kingdom more prosperous than he found it and at peace.

When Charles II died he left no legitimate heir (though he had least fourteen illegitimate offspring) and it was his brother, James II (1633–1701), who succeeded to the throne. James was an ardent Catholic convert who made himself deeply unpopular by attempting to reintroduce Catholicism as the dominant religion of the country. Within six months of James's accession to the throne, the Duke of Monmouth, an illegitimate son of Charles II, landed with a small army brought from Holland at Lyme, Dorset, and was proclaimed King by Protestant sympathizers. The rebellion was quickly quashed but in the aftermath, when many executions and deportations took place, James II became the subject of increasing hatred amongst a large section of the population.

November 1688 saw a more decisive military incursion when William of Orange (the son-in-law of James II) landed at the head of a strong army at Torbay, Devon, at the invitation of a group of opposition leaders in despair at the

8. William of Orange and Queen Mary, depicted on a plate, probably made at Lambeth *c.* 1688–94. The couple are in their royal robes carrying insignia and wearing crowns. The noticeable use of orange pigment for the emblems of monarchy lends a symbolic touch.

intolerance of James's rule. Bloodshed was avoided in England when the King's forces fell apart due to internal dissension, but in Scotland and Ireland there was massive political dislocation. James fled into exile and in February 1689 the Convention Parliament declared the throne vacant; the succession passed to William and his consort Mary, James II's daughter, who were duly crowned. As a result of this 'Glorious Revolution', England found herself henceforth

with a monarchy of a more constitutional complexion.

William III never enjoyed the national affection extended to Mary, but he continued to rule alone for eight years after she died in 1694. His popularity was compromised by his dragging England out of her isolation and into costly conflicts on the Continent, culminating in the War of the Spanish Succession. In Ireland his role in defeating James II's troops at the Battle of the Boyne in 1690, with the ensuing subjugation of the Catholics, was so central that his name continues to symbolize the bitter divisions in that country.

When William died in 1702 he was succeeded by Queen Anne (reigned 1702–14), the last of the Stuart line to rule in Britain. The victories achieved on land by the Duke of Marlborough and at sea under Admiral Rooke during Anne's reign gave the British an international influence never before attained. It was under Anne in 1707 that the Act of Union was signed between England and Scotland, so forming the United Kingdom of Great Britain.

Queen Anne died leaving no heir (although she had borne seventeen children, none of them survived her). Under the terms of the Act of Settlement (1701) the throne was offered to the Elector of Hanover, a great-grandson of James I by the female line; in 1714 he was crowned King George I. More than fifty candidates with a closer claim in blood were excluded from the succession at this time on account of their Roman Catholicism. The Stuarts' rule over England had seen a great deal of turbulence and the Jacobite cause continued to be a source of disaffection and even open hostility for decades to come. It was the House of Hanover that was to endure, however, while the Stuart line was destined to expire in exile.

Puritans, Separatists and Religion in the Seventeenth Century

The reformation of the Church in England had progressed piecemeal and to some extent fortuitously, but by the end of the sixteenth century Queen Elizabeth ruled a country that was effectively a Protestant nation. Nevertheless there were extremes of belief within the Christian community in England. The reform movement identified with the Puritans sought to 'purify' the Church of England from any sign of Roman Catholic observance, while at the other end of the spectrum the Catholics refused to acknowledge any religious authority but that of the Pope. The seeds of Puritanism first flourished in a controversy over ritual, vestments and the use of a prescribed liturgy; later the movement became more radical, seeking to abolish the episcopacy.

Initially Elizabeth had shown a degree of tolerance towards Catholics. The title of Supreme Governor of the Church of England, conferred on her by the Act of Supremacy of 1559 proved more acceptable to Catholics than that of Supreme Head and held out the prospect of conciliation. On the other hand, the Act of Uniformity asserted that Cranmer's Prayer Book, written in English and incorporating much Protestant doctrine, was to be used in every parish church, a move greatly pleasing to the Puritans.

James I inherited from Elizabeth the problem of balancing demands from Puritans and Catholics alike. Both parties expected much of their new king, and both had their hopes dashed. James's original decision to abolish fines imposed upon religious recusants (those who did not conform to the practices and observances of the Established Church) was quickly reversed and even heavier taxes than previously were imposed. This move (although prompted by economic

9. Communion cups, c. 1600. A huge amount of medieval church plate was melted down after the Reformation and converted into communion cups of this type. Wealthier churches might also commission matching flagons and alms dishes as well.

10. James II while Duke of York, by John Riley. James was never widely popular, owing to his strongly held Catholic beliefs.

considerations) became one of the principal causes for the Gunpowder Plot.

In 1605 a group of Catholics led by Robert Catesby conspired to blow up the Houses of Parliament. Their alleged aim was to kill over 300 Protestant members along with the King, to take over the government and to restore Catholicism to England. The plot was discovered and one of the conspirators, Guido (Guy) Fawkes, was arrested in the cellars where thirty-six barrels of gunpowder were discovered. The plotters were subsequently executed and their actions severely harmed the Catholic cause.

On the Puritan side hopes were raised when in 1604 a special conference was called at Hampton Court. James was invited to consider a petition, said to have been signed by 1,000 clergymen, asking for a number of reforms, which, on the face of it, were not unreasonable. Indeed, the request for a new translation of the Bible was accepted, leading to the preparation of the Authorized (King James) Version (1611), the most widely read book in the English language. However, when a demand was made that bishops should be dispensed with and that the form of church government should be changed, James was incensed: the suggestion revived memories of his troubles with just such a problem in Scotland and the King was adamant in his rejection of it with the response 'No Bishop, no King'. The result of this conference was a proclamation that unless clergy were henceforth willing to conform to the existing rules of the Church service, they would be deprived of their livings. Three hundred Puritans refused and were ejected; many fled from England, most famously when in 1620 a group of them set sail for America in the *Mayflower*.

During the Civil War of the 1640s religion played a major part in dividing the country. Among Parliamentarians there was a fear of Catholic conspiracy whilst on the Royalist side there was nervousness that the Church of England would be destroyed by Puritanism. When the Parliamentarian cause prevailed its supporters had no doubt that God was on their side. During the years of Cromwell's Protectorate further religious sects were spawned and many of his original supporters tired of the growing puritanical (and political) fanaticism that seemed to threaten the traditional order of society. At this time, a variety of Separatist groups were formed, some (the Levellers and Diggers, for example) motivated by political idealism and others (the Quakers) with a religious basis. The people tired of the extremes of Puritanism and when Cromwell died they were only too ready to welcome back as king Charles II, a Protestant and an Anglican, who had resisted attempts by his mother Henrietta Maria while in exile to convert him to Catholicism. During his reign Charles attempted to extend religious toleration to his Nonconformist and Roman Catholic subjects but his policies were thwarted. There was an arousal of anti-Catholic feeling in 1678, following the

11. Guy Fawkes's lantern. A 'dark lantern' composed of two cylinders of sheet iron, it has now lost its original horn window. Given to the University in 1641 by Robert Heywood, son of a Justice of the Peace who had been present at the arrest of Guy Fawkes in the cellars of the Parliament House, when the 'Gunpowder Plot' was foiled on 5 November 1605.

Popish Plot, a scheme initiated by Titus Oates that allegedly aimed to assassinate Charles II, massacre English Protestants, overthrow the government and finally to put the Catholic James, Duke of York on the throne. The whole plot was eventually proven to be false.

When Charles II died and was succeeded by his brother James II, religious persecution returned on a large scale. Any anti-Catholic aversion to the accession of James in the aftermath of the Popish Plot was outweighed by fear of the return of republicanism and in due course James was crowned. The invasion by the Duke of Monmouth, in 1685 failed in its attempt to overthrow James and led to the execution or transportation for life of many hundreds of Dissenters. A significant section of the population bore a lasting enmity for James and his

12. Henrietta Maria, studio of Antonie van Dyck. The daughter of Henry IV of France and Marie de Médicis, she was married to Charles I at the age of fifteen. A devout Catholic, she proved herself a loyal and courageous wife during the Civil War, but in 1644 fled to France, never to see her husband again.

second wife, Mary of Modena, ever fearful of their strong Catholic sympathies; when the Protestant William of Orange landed at Torbay in 1688 he proclaimed himself the restorer of liberty and guardian of the Protestant succession. Since that time, no Catholic monarch has been permitted to reign in England.

Civil War and Parliamentary Reform

W HEN JAMES I DIED in 1625, the country had high hopes of the more personable Prince Charles, who succeeded to the throne. Charles I, however, proved less approachable than his father and distanced himself from his people, depending upon favourites like the Duke of Buckingham for advice. His choice of advisers was unfortunate and led him to make bad decisions. When Buckingham was assassinated in 1628 Charles drew closer to his (French, Roman Catholic) wife Henrietta Maria, a move which provided no relief to his political troubles, although at a personal level the couple formed a bond that hitherto had been missing from their marriage. Having been brought up in France under an absolutist monarchy, Henrietta Maria was inclined to promote her husband's autocratic tendencies and his opposition to parliamentary rule. In this context Parliament challenged Charles by drawing up a Petition of Right that had four demands: any taxes levied were to be approved by Parliament; every accused person was to have a trial; no private household should be forced to billet troops; martial law was to be abolished. Rejecting these demands, Charles dissolved Parliament in 1629 and for the next eleven years he governed without its advice (or indeed interference).

For a number of years things went well enough under Charles's 'personal rule' and his policy seemed to be vindicated, but in 1637/8 he made two mistakes. First he inappropriately levied Ship Money. The new tax was challenged

13. John Hampden's spur. Hampden was one of the five Members whose attempted arrest by King Charles in Parliament, helped to precipitate the Civil War. When Hampden was mortally wounded at Chalgrove Field on 18 June 1643, this brass spur was removed from his boot.

by John Hampden, a rich Buckinghamshire squire, who refused to pay on the grounds that such a tax had never before been levied upon inland towns and that the King had introduced it without the approval of Parliament. The case went to court and although a majority of judges found in favour of the King, Hampden became a hero for his principled stand.

Charles's second mistake was to order in 1637 the adoption of a version of the English Prayer Book in all Scottish churches. The Scots defended their religion and entered into a Covenant to support it against all attacks. With the intention of suppressing this rebellion Charles invaded Scotland in 1639 and again in 1640 faced a Scottish army that had marched into

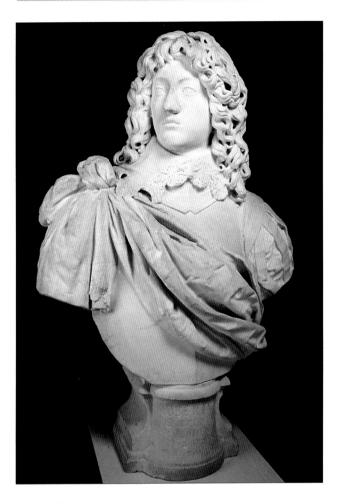

14. Bust of Prince Rupert, by François Dieussart
c. 1660. Rupert, the nephew of Charles I, was a
professional soldier experienced in warfare who, with
his daring and style, cut a romantic figure during the
Civil War.

England to meet him. On both occasions the
King's undisciplined, under-funded and unwilling
troops were reluctant to fight against a determined Scottish force; Charles had to concede the
political and religious claims of the Scots but his
campaigns had proved costly and to save himself
from bankruptcy he was obliged to recall
Parliament. The 'Long Parliament' met for the
first time on 3 November 1640 and sat in almost
continuous session until 1653, during which time
the King was forced to accept Parliament's
demands, including the execution of his most
loyal supporter, the Earl of Strafford. Many

Members of Parliament doubted Charles's ability
to keep his word and their concerns were confirmed when, in January 1642, Charles marched
into the House of Commons in an attempt to
arrest five Members who had openly criticized
him. Such a provocative action, along with
Charles's ambition to raise a force to quell rebellion in Ireland, caused offence among many
Members who were already nervous of the King's
growing control of the army and his capacity to
suppress Parliamentary rights: while they sought
the means to control the King, however, some
who had been critical of Charles now worried
that Parliament was exceeding its authority and
was set on an illegal course of action. Two dis-
tinct factions formed, Royalists for the King and
Parliamentarians against him. The country slid
into civil war when, in August 1642, Charles raised
his standard at Nottingham against his rebellious
subjects. The first major encounter took place at
Edgehill, near Banbury, where the armies of King
and Parliament were evenly matched. Although
no side could claim total victory, a cavalry charge
headed by Prince Rupert of the Rhine (1619–82),
the 23-year-old nephew of the King, saved the
day for the Royalist side. The carnage on both
sides horrified Charles and instead of pressing on
to take London, he made his base in Oxford from
1642 to 1646. The city was well placed for a march
on London and well served with rivers and roads
for communications to other areas; the university
could provide premises for housing large numbers of people; the natural position with rivers on
either side, as well as the presence of the old city
walls, meant it was easily defended, especially
when encircled by an additional ditch and earth-
work rampart. The King lodged at Christ Church
College, the Queen at Merton College; officers
and courtiers were housed at other colleges whilst
many of the ordinary soldiers were billeted on
the citizens. Charles, short of money and without
access to the mint in London, established an
alternative one in Oxford. It was only one of a
number of provincial mints set up during the
Civil War but the Oxford coins were the most
splendid. Silver plate, demanded from citizens
and colleges and sometimes reluctantly given, was
melted down to produce an exceedingly diverse
silver coinage. The most spectacular issue struck

15. Silver crown from the Oxford mint, 1644 (obverse and reverse). The coin is the work of Thomas Rawlins. Beneath the King's horse can be seen the war-time defences and a palisade as well as the spire of the University church. Rawlins may have been influenced by Wenceslaus Hollar's view of Oxford, published in 1643.

16. Dunbar Medal (reverse) by Thomas Simon, struck in gold, silver and bronze in 1650 and issued by Cromwell for services in the field at the battle of Dunbar. It is one of the earliest official military awards, showing Parliament sitting with the Speaker in his chair (the same design used by Simon for the Great Seal).

17. Cromwell's death-mask. This plaster image was cast from one of a number of wax impressions taken at the time of his death. During his lying in state, Cromwell's body was represented by a wooden effigy with wax features; after the Restoration one of these waxen effigies was ritually hanged by the neck from a window in Whitehall.

18. Bradshaw's hat, as worn at the trial of the King. A professional lawyer, Bradshaw held strong views and was determined to administer his office as President of the Court, in spite of assassination threats against which he had this hat specially made. It is of leather and is lined with steel plates, which have been exposed through wear and tear.

was the Oxford crown, the only English coin ever to feature identifiable scenery: it depicts the King on horseback riding over a panoramic view of the city, including certain recognizable landmarks as well as the fortifications built with the aid of the citizens and undergraduates. On the reverse of these coins, in abbreviated Latin, are spelled out the objectives embraced by the King, namely to defend the Protestant Religion, the laws of England and the freedom of Parliament – exactly equivalent to the declared aims of the Parliamentarians.

Early engagements, from 1642 to 1644, revealed a lack of discipline in the armies of both sides. Oliver Cromwell, a captain in the Parliamentary army, determined that more professional training was called for. He created a well-drilled force, the New Model Army, which at the battle of Naseby in 1645 was victorious against the might of the cavalry of Prince Rupert. From that time the King's cause was doomed and in 1646 he fled to the Scots and Oxford gave way to the Parliamentarians. He was given over to Parliament at Holmby, Northamptonshire, in 1647, and in spite of a series of Royalist risings in various parts of the country the King's fate was sealed; eventually he was brought to London and tried before a self-appointed 'High Court' in Westminster Hall, presided over by John Bradshaw. Charles refused to recognize the court or to offer a plea against the charge of treason. The court took his silence as an admission of guilt and accordingly sentence of death was passed on 27 January 1649. Three days later King Charles was beheaded in public outside the Banqueting House, in Whitehall.

Hostilities did not end even at this point (with major engagements still to come at Dunbar in 1650 and at Worcester in 1651), but the battles fought by Prince Charles (now Charles II, although unrecognized by Parliament) and his army of Scots ended in overwhelming successes for Cromwell's Roundheads. The Monarchy was abolished, as was the House of Lords, but the purged 'Rump' of the Parliament that took over the running of the country seemed to many little better than what had gone before and in 1653 Cromwell, backed by the army, dismissed the Parliament declaring that henceforth he would rule personally as Lord Protector.

Life under the Commonwealth was shaped by the Puritans and was not to everyone's liking. When Cromwell died in 1658 and his son proved a feeble leader, the decision was taken to restore the Stuart line to the throne. Charles II returned to London on 29 May 1660 and his accession was formally recognized with his coronation at Westminster on 23 April 1661 – an occasion met with general rejoicing on the part of the populace.

Settlement and Trade

D URING THE STUART PERIOD a transfor-
mation took place in the status of England
amongst the other European powers, attributable
to her growing influence through trade. In spite of
the success of Sir Francis Drake against Spain,
neither that country nor France nor even the
Dutch considered Elizabethan England to be any-
thing other than a backward and uncivilized
nation. Until the accession of James I in 1603, the
English continued to profit from piracy in waters
adjacent to the North American coastline. James I
disapproved of piracy, however, and signed an
Anglo-Spanish peace treaty which led to a new
era of security at sea.

Piracy had proved more lucrative and less dif-
ficult to sustain than attempting to settle a perma-
nent community in Virginia – a project attempted
during Elizabeth's reign but one that had failed
dismally. Under James, the idea was promoted
that America would yield fabulous returns in raw
materials and trade, and that it formed a sound
business prospect. Consequently settlement was
begun in earnest, with a view to unlocking the
riches of the continent.

A charter signed by James I in 1606 founded
the Virginia Company, which was to establish an
English settlement in the Chesapeake region on
the American east coast. In 1607, the Company,
drawn mainly from London merchants, funded a
group of 108 settlers to establish the community
that was to become Jamestown on the banks of a
river that was similarly named for the King. The
site proved an unhealthy one and at first attacks

by Native Americans combined with serious food
shortages resulted in high mortality rates. Many
of the settlers were classified as gentlemen,
unused to hard labour; they were motivated (as
were their sponsors) by the prospect of quick

19. Tobacco box, London *c.* 1680 The exceptionally fine
engraving on this box may be associated with Simon
Gribelin. Tobacco found almost overnight favour from
its first introduction around 1588. Silversmiths were
called upon to create stylish boxes for the customers
who indulged in the new habit, while the earliest pipes
were made of clay and had very small bowls, reflecting
the high cost of the tobacco.

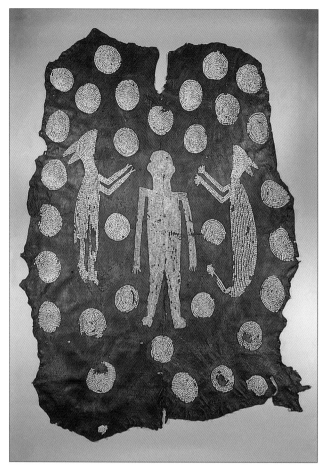

21. Gold five-guinea piece, with elephant mint-mark, 1668. A fine example of the milled coinage introduced in the reign of Charles II. The new denomination took its name from the Guinea Coast, the source of the gold imported to England by the Company of Royal Adventurers Trading to Africa, replaced in 1672 by the Royal Africa Company. Both organizations profited from the slave trade.

20. 'Powhatan's Mantle', perhaps a temple hanging associated with Powhatan, the principal adversary of Captain Smith and the father of Pocahontas. First recorded in 1638 by a visitor to the Tradescant museum in Lambeth as 'the robe of the King of Virginia', it is the most precious artefact from the earliest phases of the Jamestown Settlement.

profits through trade and were ill-adapted to growing food for survival. Under these circumstances, the famines which struck repeatedly at the early settlers were almost an inevitability. Eventually, with the encouragement and leadership of Captain John Smith, the colony achieved stability, in some measure due to the successful growing of Indian corn (maize) but more especially because of a profitable cash crop – tobacco. The struggle to survive also involved contact with local groups of Algonquian Indians, whose leader Powhatan headed over thirty tribal communities in the coastal region of Virginia. The Powhatan Indians were hunter-gatherers as well as farmers and it was in some measure due to their help, especially that of Pocahontas, daughter of Powhatan, that the community survived. Nevertheless epidemics, internal disputes and constant quarrels with the Indians placed a heavy burden on the investors of the Virginia Company and in 1624 the crown revoked the charter of the Company and placed the colony under royal control.

It was for very different reasons that 102 passengers set sail from Plymouth on the *Mayflower* in 1620. Thirty-five of the ship's complement were radical Puritans escaping from religious persecution whilst sixty-six were from poor families driven to find betterment in the New World. The Pilgrim Fathers, as they came to be known, met many severe tests but it was they who established a settled colony in New England with its own laws and form of government, which laid the foundation for what was to become the United States. The great migration of Puritans and others continued during the reign of Charles I: hundreds became tens of thousands by the 1640s, when other settlements with their own aims were established. Maryland, for example, was a Catholic colony established in 1632.

A new chapter in the colonization of North America opened under Charles II, when, in March 1681, the King signed a charter handing over a large area to William Penn in payment of a debt owed by the King to Penn's father, Admiral Sir William Penn. The charter, which was officially proclaimed on 2 April 1681, named the territory Pennsylvania. Just as the Pilgrim Fathers had done in Plymouth, the Quakers in Pennsylvania established a community governed by principles enshrined in their own religious beliefs; they made some effort to treat the Native Americans of the region with friendship, gleaning from them in return local knowledge that aided the survival of the colony.

English influence also spread to the Atlantic islands of Bermuda, Barbados, Jamaica and elsewhere, with the intention that these islands should be used as bases for expanding trade in this region. In the Caribbean, sixteenth-century Spanish explorers had not only plundered the riches of the lands but also decimated the native population by overwork and by the introduction of European diseases. In consequence, a trade began that saw ships bringing slaves from Africa and eventually returning with cargoes of cocoa beans, sugar and tobacco. African slaves were also taken to work in the new settlements in southern North America, especially in the tobacco and cotton plantations. Thus a three-way trade was established, manufactured goods going to Africa in exchange for slaves who were then shipped to the Americas, while the returning cargoes brought raw materials and food to Britain. This circular trade proved immensely lucrative and London especially became an enormous clearing-house for the transfer of goods crossing from west to east.

England also took steps to reorganize her growing influence on the world stage and to control the growing colonies. The Navigation Act of 1660, the first of a number of such measures,

22. Silver sugar-box with scallop shell, English, early seventeenth-century. The shape was particularly popular, but the incorporation of a real shell is rare. The fact that King James was on the throne and the scallop shell is the symbol of St. James, patron saint of pilgrims, may have influenced the popularity of this motif.

declared that goods bound for England or to English colonies, regardless of origin, must be shipped only in English vessels, that three-quarters of the personnel of those ships must be Englishmen and that certain goods coming from the colonies, such as sugar, cotton, and tobacco, must be shipped only to England. Trade in those particular items with other nations was prohibited, a move that was to prove particularly restrictive for Virginia and Maryland. Those two colonies were awarded a monopoly over the English tobacco market but there was no prospect that England alone could absorb their tobacco production.

The Muscovy Company and the East India Company had each been established in Tudor times and both continued to bring wealth to the country. While the activities of the Muscovy Company remained focused on the Baltic, luxury goods from the Orient came at first from India as the East India Company set up trading stations on

23. Bead calculator or abacus. This instrument is undoubtedly a Russian *schety*, possibly brought to England by John Tradescant the elder from his visit to Archangel in 1618. There was no calculating device comparable to the *schety* in western Europe at this time and this is the oldest specimen in existence.

the Indian mainland, having been unable to overcome the strong Dutch hold on the Spice Islands in south-east Asia; by the middle of the seventeenth century, however, the East India Company was trading goods from sources stretching from Arabia to Sumatra. Throughout the seventeenth century the search for a quicker northern passage from Europe to Asia continued. Henry Hudson was funded by both the Muscovy Company and the East India Company in the voyage that resulted in 1609–10 in the discovery of the Hudson River and Hudson Bay, and ultimately in establishing a British claim on much of Canada. So it was that from being a country primarily dependent for its wealth on the wool trade, England became a world-trading nation and the more affluent members of English society gained access to goods in 1700 that their forebears in 1600 had never experienced.

Progress in the Arts

ENGLISH TASTE for the collecting of paintings and sculpture blossomed during the Stuart age, especially during the reigns of Charles I and Charles II when artistic talent found easier access to patronage. No native artist of this period could claim international stature, however, and painters such as Lely, Kneller, Rubens and Van Dyck were all of foreign origin. Growing numbers of patrons aspired to commissioning portraits of themselves and their families and if no artist of renown was affordable the services could be sought of the more talented English painters such as John Riley, William Dobson and the de Critz family to grace the walls of their houses. Miniatures continued to be popular and the work of Jean Petitot and of Samuel Cooper – probably the most gifted English artist of the period – was much sought after during the seventeenth century. Grinling Gibbons, another immigrant and the best wood carver of the seventeenth century, executed many commissions for the nobility and worked for Sir Christopher Wren on St. Paul's. Other sculptors created lively likenesses (see Fig. 50), but again the most talented practitioners were immigrants.

In the early Stuart period, many new baronetcies were created and with the ready availability of land the nobility and gentry bolstered their prestige by building new houses or improving older properties by incorporating features inspired by the continental Renaissance. One such residence was Hatfield House, in origin a medieval monastic house, later taken by Henry

24. Miniatures of Louis XIV, the Duchesse d'Aguillon and Charles II, by Jean Petitot or his circle. A painter of enamels, Petitot was employed by Charles I to copy Old Masters which might be incorporated into watches, snuffboxes etc. He also made miniature portraits based on full-size paintings. The portrait of Charles II, perhaps by an artist other than Petitot, may be based on the likeness painted by John Riley.

25. Elias Ashmole, painted by John Riley to mark the foundation of the Ashmolean Museum in 1683. Ashmole is clothed in red velvet and displays the gold chains and medals bestowed on him by royal Knights of the Garter in return for copies of his *History* of the Order, on which he rests his hand. The frame by Grinling Gibbons is a masterpiece of that carver's art.

26. Thomas Howard, 2nd Earl of Arundel, by Rubens. Arundel, characterized as 'the father of vertu in
England', shares with Charles I and the Duke of Buckingham the honour of introducing artistic connoisseurship
to England. He was one of Rubens's first patrons here: the drawing is a particularly lively image and in its
characterization of the Earl is one of Rubens's finest portrait drawings.

VIII and used as a residence for his children. James I inherited the house but was not enamoured with it and persuaded his chief minister, Robert Cecil, Earl of Salisbury, to accept it in exchange for his fine Renaissance mansion at Theobalds. Cecil set about turning Hatfield House into one of the showpieces of England, employing the finest materials and best craftsmen available. Among the latter was the gardener, John Tradescant, who, dispatched to The Netherlands to find rare plants and trees, brought back over 1,000 specimens from his first visit. The splendour of the planting at Hatfield resulted in its exerting a huge influence on gardening in England. The Duke of Buckingham and James I also patronized John Tradescant senior while his son John, later to succeed his father as Royal gardener, extended the search for rare plants with several visits to Virginia.

Inigo Jones, a designer of masques, a popular amusement at the court of James I, was also employed by the Earl of Salisbury as a designer for his entertainments at Hatfield. While visiting Italy in the company of the young Earl of Arundel, Jones fell greatly under the influence of Andrea Palladio, the great innovator who reawakened interest in classical architecture, and on his return to England he played an important role in introducing the Palladian style that came to predominate in English architecture. Among Jones's surviving architectural masterpieces are the Banqueting House at Whitehall, the Queen's House at Greenwich and Wilton House, Salisbury.

The Restoration of King Charles II heralded a period of gaiety that was reflected in new fashions at court. An important event occurring soon afterwards was to have a major (if indirect) effect on art and design. The Great Fire of London (1666) which burned for five days, not only wiped out thousands of buildings but also cleansed the city of the last major visitation of the bubonic plague which had struck during the previous year. These experiences were followed by a sense of relief that gave way to a plunge into extravagance. Some of Inigo Jones's masterworks were destroyed in the fire but it also brought benefits in facilitating the rebuilding of London as a cleaner, more open city graced by many more stone

27. Venus and Cupid, by Georg Petel. A superlative example of small-scale sculpture of the early seventeenth century. Once in Rubens's collection, it was acquired by the Duke of Buckingham, one of the great collectors of the era.

buildings. Sir Christopher Wren (1632–1723) was appointed to plan the new city but spectacular costs and vested interests combined to frustrate the implementation of his scheme. Nevertheless he was confirmed as the architect for the new St. Paul's, more than fifty churches and other important buildings. Fashionable new houses sprang up

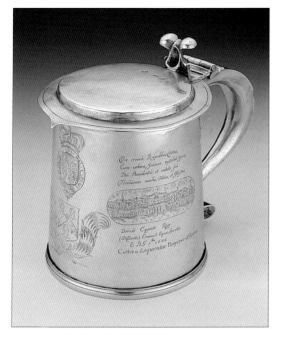

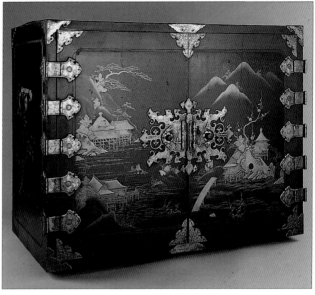

29. Lacquer cabinet, *c.* 1660. Japanese lacquer cabinets were fashionable as exotic and useful pieces of furniture. They were usually displayed in English houses on specially made gilt stands, not original to the cabinet.

28. Fire of London tankard. One of a number of silver tankards presented to his friends by Sir Edmund Berrie Godfrey, to mark both his knighthood and the gift of 800 ounces of silver from Charles II for services rendered during the Great Plague and the subsequent Fire of London. The oval panels depict the burial of victims of the Plague of 1665 and the Fire of the following year.

and demand surged for the latest styles of furnishings. A further contributory factor in promoting new design ideas in England was to come from France. In 1685 the revocation of the Edict of Nantes drove Protestant Huguenots into exile – many of them settling in Britain, especially in London. Huguenots, especially skilled as silversmiths, silkweavers, glassworkers and cabinetmakers, were able to fulfil the flourishing demand for furnishings and brought a style and finish to the decorative arts that raised standards as never before.

The interiors of rooms in the late seventeenth century adopted an entirely new appearance. Wood-panelling began to give way to walls covered with flock wallpaper or finely tooled leather; alternatively walls might be plastered and painted and further embellished with gilded carving. Some grand ceilings had painted panels, and many had elaborate mouldings and strapwork.

There was a greater variety of furniture to fill the lighter, larger rooms. The chests that stored household linen and clothes developed into chests of drawers. The open shelves of the court cupboard developed doors and became closed standing cupboards. Walnut ousted oak as the favoured wood and chairs were upholstered with the silks and brocades. What became the norm at court and the fashion of the nobles and gentry who rebuilt their houses in London soon filtered down to polite society and into the provinces.

Musicians began to be called upon to write for theatrical productions other than the popular masques. One such was Henry Purcell, a Chapel Royal chorister who became organist at Westminster Abbey, who composed the first English opera and whose popular songs were sung by soldiers during the Glorious Revolution. Following the sobriety which officialdom had attempted to impose during the Commonwealth, music and dancing could be freely enjoyed anywhere from the humble alehouse or village green, to the barber's shop and the Court.

30. Court cupboard, English, early seventeenth-century, of oak, walnut and sycamore, holly, ebony and bog-oak –
one of the finest of its kind to have survived. A label in the top drawer claims that this piece belonged to James I,
and the shields borne by the unicorn and lion uprights incorporate both the English rose and the Scottish thistle of
the Stuarts. Court cupboards developed in the late sixteenth century for use as serving tables and for the display
of cups, plate and other valuable possessions. Their name derives from the French *court*, for short.

31. Marquetry chest, *c.* 1690, typical of the furniture that came into favour in the reign of William and Mary, using walnut with decorative inlays of a variety of woods and green-stained bone. The legs are spirally turned with curved stretchers.

William Shakespeare was still the dominant force in the theatre at the beginning of the seventeenth century and in 1605/6 the first performance of *Macbeth* took place. There can be no doubt that the play was written to please King James, with its setting in Scotland and with its focus on themes such as regicide, treason and witchcraft – all very much in the forefront of the King's thoughts at that time. *The Tempest,* Shakespeare's last play (*c.* 1610), although set in Italy, contains references to strange and wild

creatures, reflecting a contemporary interest in tales from the New World.

Jacobean drama began to cater for new tastes when John Webster and others wrote revenge tragedies (e.g., *The Duchess of Malfi,* 1623), whilst Ben Jonson emerged as the master of satire (e.g. *Volpone,* 1606). The theatre declined in the period following the death of James I but poetry flourished. John Milton was the greatest writer of the mid-century (his masterpiece, *Paradise Lost,* was begun in the 1640s and not completed until

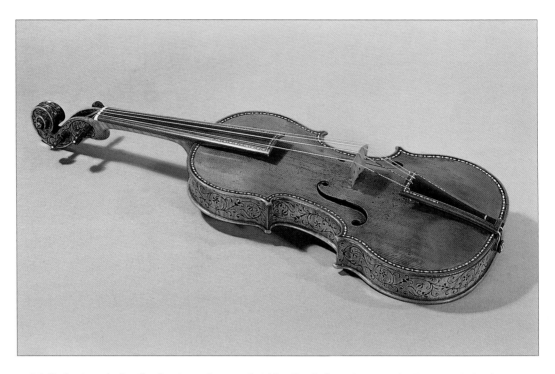

32. Violin, by Antonio Stradivarius. An early example of Stradivarius's work (*c.* 1683), its size suggests that it was made for a child. There is inlay of ivory diamond-shapes and mother-of-pearl in a flower design as well as black mastic, all combined in an extraordinary feat of craftsmanship.

after the Restoration), and John Dryden followed him writing drama (*All for Love,* 1678) and literary criticism as well as poetry. The metaphysical poets such as John Donne, who published his first verse in 1611 but many of whose works appeared only after his death in 1631, rivalled Cavalier poets like Robert Herrick (*Hesperides,* 1648).

With the Restoration in 1660 the theatres were reopened and a new period of English drama was established. Prose too had its riches in the work of John Bunyan. The diaries of Samuel Pepys and John Evelyn provide to this day an insight into life in the second half of the seventeenth century and although his great work was to come after the death of Queen Anne, Jonathan Swift was already writing during the Stuart era (*A Tale of a Tub,* 1704).

Symbols of Social Status

M ANY CHANGES TOOK PLACE in English society in the seventeenth century when a variety of new customs were adopted and novel tastes experienced. No longer totally dependent on wool, England's economic base grew substantially through her trade with the new colonies. Many of the gentry, who in earlier times had not ventured far from their rural estates, now had sufficient affluence to spend more time in the capital where new social graces and manners might be acquired. Raw materials and foodstuffs shipped to England included commodities such as tea, coffee, chocolate, sugar and tobacco to say nothing of cotton and the fine porcelains that were now finding their way from the Far East to Europe.

In London by the 1660s it was possible to purchase tea from China, coffee from Arabia and Turkey, and chocolate from the West Indies. Of all the new imports, tea brought the most far-reaching changes to social life in England, although at first it was regarded as primarily for medicinal use. Catherine of Braganza, the Portuguese princess, was already a confirmed tea drinker when she married King Charles II in 1662 and, when it was recounted that she served the new beverage at court, tea drinking became the height of fashion among aristocratic society. The Portuguese were the first Europeans to import Chinese porcelain, followed by the Dutch; adapted in shape and pattern to suit Western taste, it became as desirable as the tea to be drunk from it. When tea was first tasted in

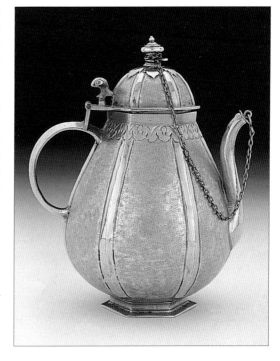

33. Teapot, by Benjamine Pyne, 1680. The first silver teapots were very small and usually based on imported Chinese or Japanese wine- or water-pots, which were gourd-shaped. Porcelain teapots were not widely available in England until production flourished in the second half of the eighteenth century.

England the only ceramic vessels locally produced were of coarse earthenware which, until the advent of fine stonewares in the later

34. Japanese tea-cup and saucer. The cup has a slightly everted lip and the saucer a foliated rim. They are painted in a Kakiemon-style palette with red lotus blooms linked with formal scrolls and leaves on the outside of the cup and inside the saucer. They date from the third quarter of the seventeenth century.

seventeenth century, were totally unsuitable to withstand the high temperatures necessary for use in this way. Along with tea, Chinese porcelains came as ballast in ships loaded with luxury goods such as silks, spices, ebony and jade. Porcelain, found to be delicate yet hard, heat-resistant and easy to clean, must have seemed incredibly refined to Europeans accustomed to earthenware. Owing to internal unrest in seventeenth-century China, export production was disrupted and the Dutch East India Company, which by then had the monopoly of this trade, turned to Japan, where porcelain to suit the European taste began to be produced. Goldsmiths, employed in making sets of equipment for the ritual presentation of tea drinking, to begin with made small teapots in the form of Chinese water-pots. Only the very wealthy would have had the means to commission silverware or to buy Chinese and Japanese

porcelain, but as the tea itself was extremely expensive (a pound of the best quality being the equivalent of a year's wages for a servant) no doubt they could afford the luxury. The new tea wares, however, seemed so fragile and the porcelain so liable to damage from the hot water that the custom arose in England of pouring a little cold milk into the bowl – a precautionary measure that developed into one of the rituals associated with tea drinking. The price of tea fell gradually and the custom of tea drinking had spread to all levels of society by the reign of Queen Anne.

Even at the time when tea was still an exotic drink for the few, coffee was already available to a wider public by the mid-seventeenth century in the new-style coffee houses. A number of Englishmen, travelling in Islamic countries, had recounted their experiences of drinking coffee some years before its first appearance in England was recorded by John Evelyn (in 1637, at Balliol College, Oxford). Its introduction to the academic community no doubt led to the opening of the first coffee house in England as described by the Oxford antiquary Anthony Wood, 'at the Angel in the parish of St. Peter's in the East' in

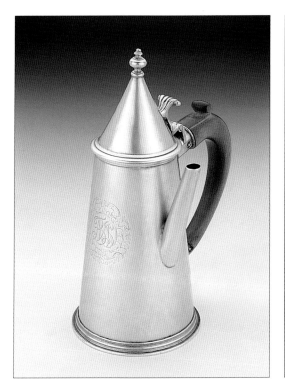

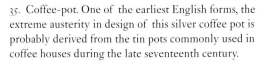

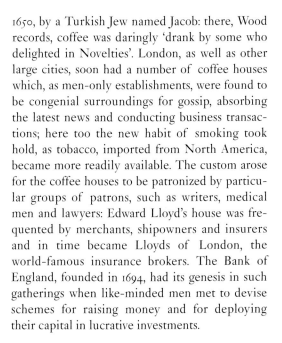

35. Coffee-pot. One of the earliest English forms, the extreme austerity in design of this silver coffee pot is probably derived from the tin pots commonly used in coffee houses during the late seventeenth century.

36. Chocolate-pot, 1696, Chocolate-pots adopted similar shapes to coffee pots but had an extra aperture in the lid: this was to enable a stirrer to be inserted to stop the chocolate from congealing and yet not to lose heat.

1650, by a Turkish Jew named Jacob: there, Wood records, coffee was daringly 'drank by some who delighted in Novelties'. London, as well as other large cities, soon had a number of coffee houses which, as men-only establishments, were found to be congenial surroundings for gossip, absorbing the latest news and conducting business transactions; here too the new habit of smoking took hold, as tobacco, imported from North America, became more readily available. The custom arose for the coffee houses to be patronized by particular groups of patrons, such as writers, medical men and lawyers: Edward Lloyd's house was frequented by merchants, shipowners and insurers and in time became Lloyds of London, the world-famous insurance brokers. The Bank of England, founded in 1694, had its genesis in such gatherings when like-minded men met to devise schemes for raising money and for deploying their capital in lucrative investments.

Chocolate too was drunk in the coffee houses and – like tea – at first was recommended by physicians as medicinally beneficial. The etiquette associated with coffee and chocolate drinking was different from that of tea and accordingly different kinds of vessels were produced. Early English coffee-pots (conical with a straight spout) probably derived from Turkish-style pots seen by travellers when they first encountered the drink. Chocolate-pots took much the same shape, but with the addition in the lid of an extra hole (also with a cover) where a wooden stirrer could be inserted. These pots, initially made of tin, began to appear in the goldsmith's repertoire when the habit of coffee and chocolate drinking developed into a widespread domestic custom.

The introduction of these drinks led to the displacement of alcohol as the only social lubricant, although it naturally remained popular and

37. The Mildmay Monteith, London 1684–5. Decorated with flat-chased chinoiserie ornament, this wine-glass cooler must have been the height of fashion in Charles II's reign. The 'Monteith' is a bowl with a crenellated rim, each indentation designed to hold the stem of a wine-glass while its bowl hung down in the iced water below. Believed to be named after a Scotsman who at that time wore the bottom of his coat so notched.

was indeed regarded as a necessity for the poorer classes who could not afford tea, coffee or chocolate. Ale continued to be drunk in large quantities and at a penny a quart provided cheap nourishment as well as helping to ease the hardships of daily life for the labouring poor. For the wealthier members of society the quality of wine was greatly improved when glass bottles became widely available (see fig. 48); these squat, thick green glass containers displaced the German stoneware or delftware vessels that had been used to dispense wine from barrel to table. It was observed that the wine was improved when stored in these bottles, and with the introduction of corks late in the seventeenth century it was found to last longer too. Gentlemen, tavern owners and corporate bodies began to own quantities of bottles emblazoned with their own particular crest or initials.

Until the Stuart period, fine drinking glasses had been imported from Venice to supply the needs of the court and those wealthy enough to

afford them. A new kind of lead glass, however, was perfected by George Ravenscroft and, as early as 1685, the first wine- glasses with baluster stems were being made. The English glass industry found itself amongst the most advanced in Europe, its products having a clear brilliance and sturdiness not found in Venetian soda glass and, being less costly to produce, was soon within the pocket of those of modest means (see fig. 57).

The novelty of these exotic new drinks not only stimulated the production of improved ceramics and glass but was to change the whole tenor of eating at home. The large central hall where the whole household lived and ate together had already disappeared from contemporary architecture, and as eating became a more private activity a new prominence was given to the importance of a well-equipped table in a specially designated dining room. Ceramic plates were not yet commonly used, but guests became accustomed to their host providing them with sets of cutlery, instead of having to supply their

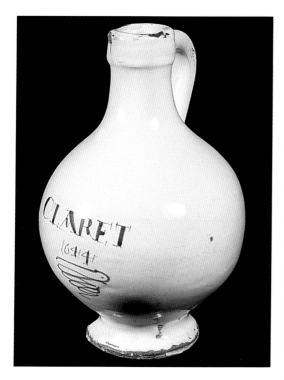

38. Delft claret-jug, 1644. These vessels, probably made in London factories and always of the same traditional shape, competed with Rhenish stoneware bottles during the late 1670s. Usually inscribed in blue with either 'Sack', 'Claret' or 'Whit[e]', they were often dated and may have been given as New Year or Christmas gifts.

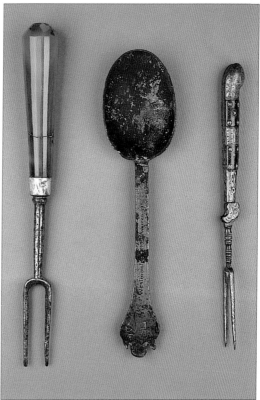

39. Two forks and a spoon. Early forks, with long stems and two straight prongs, were used only for holding the meat while it was cut and not for eating. Before they became common the traveller might carry his own fork with him. Shown here is one fork with an attractive agate handle and another with a folding handle – handy for the fastdious traveller. Spoons of base metal predominated until this time; the bowl was commonly fig-shaped while after 1630 the rod-like stem with a decorative finial became flattened with a trefid end.

own. A major change was represented by the introduction of the fork, at first a small two-pronged utensil with which meat or sweetmeats could be selected before being transferred to the fingers – but not yet directly to the mouth. Later a three-pronged variety was developed and eventually, in the eighteenth century, four prongs became customary. Spoons, meanwhile, changed little in shape and size from the sixteenth century. Salt-cellars, on the other hand, were increasingly made as small individual containers rather than the large ceremonial items that had dominated dining tables since the late Middle Ages.

Other small items of domestic silver appeared at this period – tankards, beakers, saucers, sugar-castors, porringers, wine-glass coolers, candle-sticks and even bedpans and bellows. Inventories

of the time reveal a growing number of people owning plate but those who could not afford silver might enhance their tables with the soft sheen of English pewter, a desirable alternative, that glowed in the candlelight on the dark oak furniture of the period. There can be little doubt that England, during Stuart era, experienced slow but fundamental changes in society, in which a major feature was the gradual spread of wealth to a wider sector of the population.

Craft and Industry

THROUGHOUT THE STUART ERA an economy prevailed that remained largely pre-industrial in character; that is to say, it remained essentially aristocratic and agrarian. Only the most tentative steps were taken at this time towards the mechanization of manufacturing processes: while water and wind power continued to drive rural grain mills, little impact was made on industrial production beyond the introduction of the tilt hammer and of rolling and slitting mills (the latter for cutting sheet metal into strips for the manufacture of nails, etc.) into the iron industry.

Perhaps the most far-reaching change to the industrial landscape involved the rise of coal as the principal fuel for a range of processes (not least in the glass and pottery industries considered below) at the expense of wood. Consequent on this change, the importance of certain production areas (such as the Weald), which had been heavily dependent on timber, began to decline, while the coal-rich areas of the Midlands took their first steps towards the huge expansion they were to enjoy during the Industrial Revolution. The fortunes of the North-East, and especially of Newcastle upon Tyne as the centre of the coastwise coal trade to London and the South-East, made considerable progress at this time.

As in previous centuries, the market for English products remained essentially a domestic one. English woollen cloth had long been well regarded on the Continent, but the ambitions of, for example, the Levant Company to open up new export markets were largely thwarted, with the result that their operations remained heavily

40. Wool-weight (14 pounds), cast with the Stuart arms and stamped C.B. (perhaps for the City of Bristol).

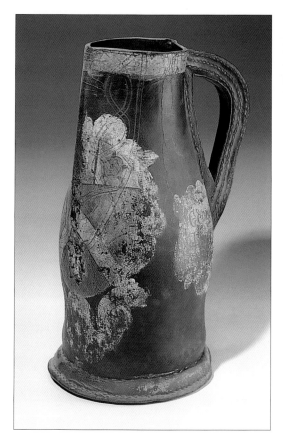

41. Blackjack or leather jug blazoned with the arms of the Joiners' Company of Oxford and dated 1712.

42. Lead seal of the South Seas and Fisheries Co. One of a number of joint stock companies set up under the later Stuarts, its spectacular collapse in the infamous South Sea Bubble followed in the reign of George I.

biased towards imports. Domestic investors continued to prefer land to commerce, although by the end of the century joint stock companies were beginning to offer tempting alternatives – although there were plenty who got their fingers burnt while speculating in this volatile market.

Wool rather than iron remained the commodity around which the economy pivoted. Traditional broadcloths (as woven, for example, in the West Country) and worsteds (an East Anglian speciality) each retained their share of the market, but the 'new draperies' produced especially around Essex and Suffolk, often by immigrant weavers, introduced a range of lighter materials to compete with light woollens and linen. Cotton, introduced by the 'Turkey Merchants' of the Levant Company, began to be spun in Lancashire from around 1600, though at first it was invariably combined with a linen weft.

Silk too became increasingly available – not due to James I's ambitious scheme to promote a domestic silk industry by encouraging the planting of mulberry trees (and here we may mention John Tradescant's appointment under Charles I as 'Keeper of His Majesty's Gardens, Vines and Silk-Worms'), but rather from the efforts of the East India merchants who imported the raw silk on a considerable scale. Commonly this would be spun in coastal centres such as Canterbury and Sandwich before being sent up to London for dying and selling-on, every stage of this process being dominated by Huguenot merchants.

The leather industry, although less well documented than textile manufacturing, was also of major importance. In some parts of the country at least, the value attached to hides can be gauged by the fact that in the seventeenth century the cattle trade was controlled by the leather workers rather than the butchers. A series of specialists was involved, starting with the skinners who separated hides from carcasses, and the tanners who undertook the long process of curing the skins (a year being the normal processing time for cattle hides); so noxious were the latter's yards with

43. Queen Anne's new wine gallon introduced in 1707 when the customary gallon was established as the official measure.

their evil-smelling tan-pits full of hides, that they were frequently banished to the fringes of the town – usually on the down-river side. After the attentions of the leather dressers, who finished hides for sale to the trade, they would be sold-on to a multiplicity of specialists including the saddlers, cordwainers or shoemakers, glovers, etc.

The gradual spread of wealth to the middling classes and the resulting increase in demand for fashionable clothing brought a reasonable level of prosperity to these craftsmen under the Stuarts. Other trades such as the horners, continued to process cattle horn into a variety of products including combs and spoons but in other areas found themselves increasingly under pressure from the expanding glass industry in the selling of

beakers, lantern and window panes, and the like, all of which had formerly been made of horn.

While the smelting of iron was practised more widely from the early decades of the seventeenth century, the manufacturing industries remained dispersed. Cast-iron fire-backs continued as a staple of the Wealden industry but most of the necessities of everyday life – plough-shares, horse-shoes, fire-irons, locks and hinges, nails, etc. – continued to be wrought by black-smiths. Some progress in specialization can be detected, however, in the formation of new trade guilds such as the clockmakers, gunsmiths and tin-plate workers, while the spread of tobacco smoking led to the emergence of specialist clay pipe makers to satisfy the demand.

Two Industrial Success Stories:
Pottery and Glass

A T THE BEGINNING of the seventeenth century, potters – on the whole – worked at or near their dwellings carrying on their craft much as they had done since the Middle Ages, with limited opportunity for long-distance trade or export. The needs of small communities as served by most potters were confined to basic household vessels, but the growing volume of imports of both Chinese and Japanese porcelains with their supreme decorative techniques and colour created a demand that encouraged English potters to develop their skills and to begin the process that was to make England's ceramic industry the leader in Europe by the middle of the eighteenth century.

The production of English delftware, introduced in the last decades of the sixteenth century, flourished in the seventeenth century when many potteries were established in centres such as London, Bristol, Liverpool and Wincanton. Using tin from Cornwall for the glaze and later introducing metal oxides to create a range of colours (other than the cobalt blue which had dominated the ware in the first years of production), the potteries required capital and administrative capacities beyond those available to a family workshop. Gradually, from about 1620 onwards, the delftware potteries increased their range of wares from the apothecaries' drug-jars that predominated in the early years to include more decorative items such as commemorative plates, dishes and chargers. The passion for blue-and-white Oriental porcelain – especially in the reign of William and

44. Delft charger, (probably Lambeth *c.* 1680–90). The combination of carnations and tulips suggests some influence from Isnik pottery of the sixteenth and seventeenth century. From about 1670 onwards, large numbers of tulip-dishes were made, some of which are among the finest achievements of the English potter.

Mary (the latter being a great collector of porcelain and of Dutch delft) – encouraged the English potters to copy designs from Chinese wares. Turkish pottery from Isnik, painted with brilliant

46. Stoneware tankard, made in London during the seventeenth century, and embellished with a silver lid, indicating that this type of pottery was highly prized.

45. Salt-glazed stoneware bottle, English, with medallion of cockerel and initials H.C., made at Dwight's Fulham pottery, London. This is one of a number of bottles so marked for Henry Crosse, proprietor of 'The Cock ale-house' next to Temple Bar, London. Found in Oxford.

colours and frequently incorporating motifs derived from China, was also an inspiration to English delftware potters. Tin-glazed earthenware, however, is very soft and not suitable for heavy daily use or for receiving the boiling water necessary for tea, so it had its limitations. Until the advent of the first English porcelain factories in the second half of the eighteenth century, the demand for more durable ceramics was supplied by salt-glazed stoneware.

    The story of English stoneware is a fascinating one that tells of men who were experimenters, scientists and entrepreneurs, of litigation, intrigue, secrets stolen and the establishment of family

dynasties that laid the foundations of one of the leading ceramic industries of Europe. In about 1672, in King Charles II's reign, John Dwight (c. 1635–1703), a trained chemist and ceramic enthusiast, embarked on a new career with the aim of commercially reproducing both fine china, as imported from the East, and also the non-porous salt-glazed stoneware vessels that had long been brought to England from the Rhineland. By 1675 Dwight had achieved remarkable success and was able for the first time to establish the manufacture of this material at Fulham, on the western fringes of London. Stoneware bottles were produced there in large quantities, following the techniques evolved in the Rhineland: these relied on the use of clays capable of being fired to temperatures in excess of 1,200°C, and the introduction of salt at a high temperature which combined with the silica in the clay to produce an impermeable coating. Imported flagons, popularly known as greybeards or Bellarmines, had face-masks applied to the necks, but Dwight soon abandoned these for ornamental medallions, often alluding to the names of wine-taverns, inns or ale-houses – The Mermaid, The Cock, etc.; heraldic badges and arms appear on others. These required moulds to be made by specialist craftsmen and hence a further division of labour.

Further away from Cornish tin but already producing on a considerable scale, the Staffordshire potteries began to experiment further with the salt glaze introduced by John Dwight. Geography, geology and timing combined to make Staffordshire the place where pottery-making began to develop on an industrial scale by the second half of the seventeenth century. North Staffordshire had the clay to make the pots and coal to fire them; the potters of the district were experienced in traditional skills and open to new ideas. The pottery towns were centrally placed to import materials from other parts of the country and to export their wares to a wide area.

As the demand for Staffordshire pottery grew, more decorative wares began to appear. Slipwares, which had been made in Kent for a number of years were further developed by the most famous of slipware potters, Thomas Toft (died Stoke-on-Trent, 1689). Working in the Restoration period, Toft's themes were frequently commemorative. Buff or reddish clay was used for the body of the dishes and covered with a layer of cream or white slip which formed the background for the trailing of slips in contrasting colours.

It was the coming of the Elers brothers to Staffordshire that was to catapult the industry into national and international notice. David and Philip Elers had worked for Dwight in Fulham and having been trained in pottery, silversmithing and chemistry were in an advantageous position to take production on to new levels. They first produced a red stoneware, reminiscent of Chinese imports; these pots could withstand heat in a way that English pottery had so far failed to do. Decoration was devised by the use of sprigging – reliefs in the form of leaves and flowers applied to the surface of the pot.

White salt-glazed wares, developed by the introduction of lighter clays from Devon, proved popular rivals to imported porcelain in their pale colours, their delicacy and their cheapness. Thomas and John Wedgwood were amongst the earliest users of salt-glazing; their success established the fortunes of one of Staffordshire's most famous ceramic dynasties.

47. Thomas Toft charger, with trailed decoration incorporating the maker's name and two aristocratic figures (perhaps even royalty). The naïve images characteristic of slipware dishes belies the technical skills involved in the production of these wares.

Stoneware bottles, used for serving wine at table after it had been taken from the cask, soon felt competition from the growing glass bottle industry. The production of bottle glass began in the closing years of the sixteenth century but resulted at first in only fragile, pale green containers. Wine bottles are mentioned in household accounts by the 1630s, by which time they were of a thicker, darker material. In 1636 an Act was passed forbidding the sale of wine by bottle in an attempt to regulate the measure of wine received by the customer: no two bottles could be blown exactly alike at this time and considerable discrepancies occurred. The Act required that the vintner should keep his wine in the cask, so that private individuals could have their bottles filled from a regular-sized butt. The Act had more profound effects, however, leading to an increase in the use of personal wine bottles and the practice of 'sealing' bottles for private use, for with so many bottles circulating at the vintner's for filling it was clearly desirable to have them marked.

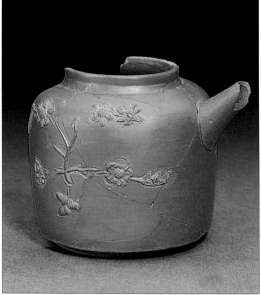

48. Glass wine-bottles. Typical sealed wine bottles of the period used for carrying wine from the cask to the table. The seals identify them as having belonged to the Three Tuns Tavern in Oxford. The shaft-and-globe form on the left dates to the mid seventeenth century and the onion-shaped bottle on the right has a dated seal of 1715.

49. Elers red stoneware teapot, showing the sprigged relief for which this thinly potted ware was celebrated, inspired by and copied from the unglazed red porcelain made in China at Yi-hsing in the seventeenth century. The stoneware fabric produced by the Elers brothers signalled the start of a new era in English ceramics.

Samuel Pepys 'visited Mr. Rawlinson's at the Mitre Tavern' where he watched some five or six dozen of his newly made sealed bottles filled with wine. He buried them during the Great Fire and retrieved them ten days later.

By 1677 bottle making had become a separate part of the glass industry. Bottles could be purchased direct from the glasshouse, ordered from the local vintner or obtained from one of the pedlars at 3s. 6d. a dozen plain, 5s. sealed. From around 1623 advances in glass-making came about due to the diminishing use of (increasingly scarce) wood from forests and the resulting use of coal as a fuel. The industry was run on a monopolistic basis, but the result was better management and development, such as the benefits of using a fuel that burned at a much higher temperature. Innovation in furnace techniques led certain glass-makers to aspire to produce a glass superior to the dark metal suitable for bottle-making, the main activity of glasshouses. However it was a chemist, George Ravenscroft, who convinced the Glass Sellers' Company that he could provide them with clear, strong lead-glass to replace the more fragile soda-glass for drinking vessels. In his glasshouse at Henley-on-Thames in 1674 he produced a fine, clear glass with a higher proportion of lead oxide which had the attractive quality of weight combined with suitability for engraving. Within a few years this type of drinking glass met all the demands of the home market.

The climate of innovation in industry increased the prosperity of merchants, industrialists and tradesmen while the advance of financial institutions helped to create the climate at the end of the seventeenth century that was to lead to the first Industrial Revolution in the following century.

The New Learning and the Expansion of Education

THE ADVANCES ALREADY NOTED in social life, in exploration, in industry and in the wealth of the nation as compared with the sixteenth century were also apparent in wider opportunities for education. During the reigns of James I and Charles I many grammar schools were founded and others were expanded. The growing wealth among the merchant class and the middle ranks of society helped to endow such schools and to fund scholarships for clever boys aspiring to the universities. The growth of literacy alongside the availability of books and pamphlets written in English opened up possibilities for those who in the past had been unable to benefit from a higher education.

The elementary or 'petty' schools instructed children in reading, writing, arithmetic and basic grammar; many children would have gone no further, but the most fortunate progressed from here to a grammar school education. Petty schools were established frequently by public-spirited persons but might also be founded by an indigent scholar or a widow who could scratch a living by providing a rudimentary education for local parishioners. In this way, as more primary schools were opened, it became more widely accepted that the poor should also receive some education, especially those destined for trades where a degree of literacy was an advantage. Of course there was the added bonus that religious texts might bring benefits and solace to the less well-off members of society. Not everyone supported education for poor children, however: many of

them remained illiterate and the great majority would have expected to be in employment – apprenticed to a master if they were lucky – by the age of eight.

Latin continued to be the language of international scholarship, but a growing need was perceived for boys to be taught to express themselves in their own language and perhaps to learn some history and geography: private schools were established to do just that. Nonconformists were excluded from the universities of Oxford and Cambridge and a few schools were set up specifically to give a higher education to such students.

The universities gradually widened their intake to include more of the nobility and gentry in colleges along with their core population of poor would-be clerics. Although the set curricula remained largely unchanged, with logic, rhetoric and the classical texts still predominating, individual tutors encouraged the study of mathematics, astronomy, history, French and Italian. Scientific subjects were not formally studied in the early seventeenth century, but to some extent their principles were introduced into other courses. Scientific research blossomed as the century progressed, when educated men across Europe exchanged ideas and learned from each other. William Harvey, who discovered the circulation of the blood, studied under Galileo Galilei at the University of Padua, where the medical teaching was the best in the world.

In 1660 the earliest learned society in Great Britain was founded, in London – the Royal

50. Sir Christopher Wren, by Edward Pierce. This marble bust captures the young Wren who was fast establishing himself as one of the great geniuses of his age.

Society 'for Improving Natural Knowledge'. It grew out of the meetings of a group of thinkers who met informally for discussions on scientific subjects at Oxford and at Gresham College in London, later receiving a royal charter in 1662. Perhaps because several of its earliest fellows were Puritans, the Royal Society gained little more than moral support from the crown. Christopher Wren, natural philosopher, astronomer and architect (who wrote the preamble to its charter), although exceptionally gifted, was typical of the group in his broad range of interests. Educated at Westminster school where he first studied astronomy and constructed meteorological devices, Wren became interested in physiology, leading him to construct models and draw detailed diagrams – practical skills that were to complement his other talents. In 1661 he was elected Savilian professor of astronomy at Oxford and in 1669 was appointed Surveyor of Works to Charles II, but it is as an architect that he is best remembered. An invitation to design the Sheldonian Theatre at Oxford gave Wren the opportunity to combine his wide scientific and mathematical interests with his art as a draughtsman and model-maker. He had already been consulted about renovating St. Paul's Cathedral before 1666 when the Great Fire of London reduced two-thirds of the City to ruins, giving him the opportunity to design an entirely new Cathedral; the rebuilding of St. Paul's took thirty-five years.

Throughout these years Wren remained in close contact with the Royal Society. Other distinguished fellows of this period include John Wilkins (1614–72), Bishop of Chester and later warden of Wadham College, Oxford, who published a paper on the use of hot air to provide energy on a principle given practical application in the smokejack, used to turn a roasting spit over the fire; he also sought to create a new philosophical language for the world of scientific inquiry. Robert Hooke (1635–1703), the Society's curator of experiments, had an equally illustrious career; his work as a chemist and physicist was to have a fundamental influence on the modern world. Sir Isaac Newton (1642–1727), English physicist and mathematician, was the culminating figure of the scientific revolution of the seventeenth century.

51. Pewter inkwell with pen-holder. The strapwork decoration is typical of the Stuart era and inkwells of this form are common accompaniments in scholarly portraits of the period.

His work on optics was crucial; his experiments resulted in the formulation of the law of gravitation; in mathematics, he was the originator of infinitesimal calculus. He was further appointed Warden, and later Master of the Mint, a position he held until his death.

Clothing and Accessories

I N A CENTURY so full of political upheaval, the tenor of life in Stuart England became somewhat less rigid than that of earlier times. This was especially true after the Restoration and with an evolving society came changes in clothing. The elaborate dress of the Tudor court and the stiffness of Jacobean fashion gave way to the soft satins and lace that brought the freedom of light and graceful clothes to the nobility during the later Stuart period. At the same time those of a more puritanical tendency shunned the excesses copied from the French court and continued to wear sombre dress of simple cut.

To begin with, the short trunk hose favoured by Tudor gentlemen gave way to padded knee-length breeches worn with a longer, tight-waisted doublet; both of these basic garments were to alter profoundly in the course of the seventeenth century. At the same time, stiff ruffs began first to soften and then to give way to large lace-trimmed collars; by the final decades of the century a lace cravat was fashionable. Breeches first grew longer and narrower with additional lace or ribbons at the knee, reaching nearly to the top of the boot when worn. By the reign of Charles II, as if counteracting the plainness of Cromwellian style, the decoration of the breeches became so extreme as to become skirt-like with cascades of lace and flounces, but this courtly fashion proved short-lived and after 1666 breeches settled back to an unadorned knee-length pattern. The stiff Jacobean doublet loosened and later shortened to become a jacket that revealed billows of shirt at the waist. By

the final years of the century the short jacket had evolved into a knee-length, multi-buttoned frock-coat, over which was worn a top-coat of similar cut. These two garments were to become the basic coat and waistcoat of a man's wardrobe for the following two centuries and beyond.

Ladies had little scope to change skirt-length since ankles were always covered, but profiles altered dramatically. A woman in the time of James I might still wear a stiff farthingale to exaggerate waist and hips, but as in the case of male practice, dress began to soften and skirts hung more loosely. Trimmings and novel ways of draping their skirts presented further opportunities for Carolean women to express their dress sense. The height of the waistline fluctuated and skirts could be cut so as to be looped back to reveal an embroidered petticoat. Bodices, cut separately from the skirt, could be fastened at either front or back and there was a multitude of ways to enhance sleeves or collars or to stiffen the front with a stomacher. Collars changed from the ruff or stiff stand-up collar (sometimes worn together) to become softly draped and shawl-like. Necklines were usually low-cut and revealing, offering opportunities for the wearing of brooches and bows to draw in the collar as modestly as the lady might require. Sleeves were on the whole three-quarter length and might be trimmed with cuffs to match the collar; extra ruffles could be added, or a little of the sleeves of a smock worn as an undergarment might be revealed.

52. Hester Tradescant with her stepson John, painted in 1645 and attributed to Thomas de Critz. Both mother and son are in fashionable seventeenth-century dress, Hester wearing a white lace-edged cap under a tall black hat with a wide brim. Her dark grey dress parts below the bodice to reveal a white under-dress embroidered with red sprigs. The fashion for lace is evident in her deep white collar. John also has a broad white collar worn outside his short jacket.

53. Virginal, London, 1670, by Adam Leversidge. When fully cased, this instrument appears as an oblong chest hinged along the front and back. The entire inside of the box is decorated with the front panels and the inside of the lid showing landscape scenes with ladies and gentlemen wearing the fashions of the period. The men are in the long skirted jackets and the high-heeled shoes popular at the time.

The Stuart period conjures up images of wide hats, a profusion of lace, ribbon and feathers, and bucket-topped boots. It is as much for accessories of this kind as for the basic dress that the era is remembered.

Short hairstyles in the reign of James I gave way to longer locks under Charles I and from the time of the Restoration no gentleman of fashion would be seen in public without his long curly wig. This custom, which came from France, swept throughout England when Charles II and his brother James, Duke of York started to wear periwigs. The first wigs, made of human hair, were very costly, and as demand increased the hair from horses and goats was increasingly used. Having the head shaved in order to wear a wig meant that hair need not be washed but wigs had to be maintained; wealthier men would own two or more, wearing one whilst the others were cleaned at the wigmaker's. Less affluent members of society bought second-hand wigs discarded by their original owners, or otherwise wore their hair long and rather straggly.

The high narrow-brimmed hats of the early seventeenth century gave way to styles with lower crowns and wider brims, made of soft felt with the brim cocked-up at one side, leaving space for a large curling feather. Less image-conscious merchants or Puritan types would have continued to wear plainer headgear, as epitomized in the black beaver hats with tall sugar-loaf crowns and stiff brims, a style worn by both sexes. When

54. Wig-curlers were part of the equipment needed to maintain a gentleman's wig, which might have cost as much as a complete outfit; therefore much attention was lavished on it from a hairdresser when it would be cleaned, curled and powdered.

55. English delftware tea-caddy decorated with a gentleman on one side and a lady on the other, both in the fashionable dress of the period.

indoors, a woman might wear a lace-trimmed linen cap, retained when she put on her outdoor clothes to show beneath her beaver hat or hidden when she wore a hood.

Gloves, originally worn to protect the hands, had taken on increasingly symbolic overtones with the passage of time to the point where they became an essential part of the costume of those in authority. By the seventeenth century, however, gloves had become a popular accessory, now larger and more decorative in character. The gauntlet glove was fashionable for both ladies and gentlemen, giving much scope for embroidery and other trimmings. Gloves could be made in one piece, but sometimes the gauntlet was made separately.

As a boy Charles I suffered from rickets and the brass supports he had to wear were disguised under specially designed boots. Although the supports became redundant in adult life, Charles continued to wear boots with the result that tightly fitting boots became the mode, also providing additional opportunities for decoration in the folded-back deep tops, lined with silk or filled with lace. By the time men were wearing the long-skirted jacket in the last quarter of the century, the preference had changed to shoes with

fairly high heels, sometimes in a contrasting colour.

There seemed to be no garment that could not be enhanced with a drape of fine white lace – even ceremonial armour, as can be seen in portraits of the period (Figs. 6 & 10). The finest lace was imported from Flanders and France but the revocation of the Edict of Nantes in 1685 brought many Huguenot lace-workers to England. The embryonic native lace industry benefited by absorbing ideas from the newcomers and it was at this period that a luxury silk industry was established in Spitalfields. With such fine accessories enhancing costume, it is not surprising that garments were bequeathed in wills or sold to be bought second-hand by the less well-off.

The Stuart Twilight

W HEN JAMES II FLED to France with his family in 1688, a good many Englishmen were pleased to welcome a king from the Protestant (if not Anglican) faith. William of Orange, with his popular wife Mary, daughter of the exiled James II, succeeded to the throne in 1689; within five years, however, Queen Mary had died of smallpox, aged only thirty-two. William proved an able monarch though little loved –

56. Bonnie Prince Charlie's Garter insignia. Even in exile the Stuarts continued to award themselves the honours dispensed by the British monarchy.

especially in Ireland and in Scotland, where politics and religion had combined to produce a violent and divided society, an element of which retained an allegiance to James II. As a means of forestalling rebellion, William ordered that every clan must swear an oath of allegiance to him before New Year's Day in 1692 or suffer savage reprisals. Most succumbed, though very reluctantly, to this threat; the harshness with which retribution was meted out to those who failed to comply further alienated the Highland clans and strengthened their loyalty to the exiled Stuarts.

On his arrival in France with his second (Roman Catholic) wife, Mary of Modena, and their newly born son, James Francis Edward, James II was warmly welcomed by Louis XIV. James's daughters by his first marriage to Anne Hyde were to come to the throne of England in turn – first Mary with her husband William of Orange, and then Anne, who was to succeed King William in 1702. Since Mary had been childless and all of Queen Anne's children had died in infancy, the Stuarts had a strong case to reclaim the throne of England and Scotland at the demise of Anne in 1714. James II had also died by this time (in 1701) and adherents to the Jacobite cause (including, Louis XIV) now acknowledged his son as James VIII of Scotland and III of England. Jacobite confidence enjoyed a boost at this time but hope of an early restoration to the throne of the Stuart line was to come to nothing. Under the Act of Settlement (1701), James was ruled out of the succession on account of his Roman Catholicism; the crown went instead in 1714 to

57. Jacobite wine-glass with engraved and coloured portrait of Prince Charles Edward, the Young Pretender. In spite of defeat at Culloden moor in 1746, the Jacobite cause continued to have its supporters. Wine-glasses were engraved with Jacobite symbols and mottoes with the hope no doubt, that they would stimulate loyal emotions. Prince Charles Edward is here dressed in tartan and wears the Garter insignia and a beret with a rose. Above is a banner inscribed 'Audentior Ibo' (I will go more boldly).

58. Striking clock, 1780 by James Cox of London. The Stuart arms with a supporting lion (the unicorn is missing) decorate this handsome ormolu clock-case. The clock is believed to have been made for Henry Benedict, Cardinal York, self-styled Henry IX, King of England, and the last of the Stuarts.

George, the Protestant Elector of Hanover, whose great-grandfather had been James VI and I.

Louis XIV made peace with Britain under the terms of the Treaty of Utrecht (1713) and the Stuart claimant to the throne, James III, was forced to leave France, eventually settling in Rome. Successive plots and attempted invasions (most notably in 1715) failed to win back his inheritance. His marriage to a Polish princess, Clementina Sobieska, produced two sons, Charles Edward (1720–88) and Henry Benedict

(1725–1807), thus keeping alive the hopes of the many exiled Jacobites who kept faith with the 'Old Pretender'.

Prince Charles Edward, popularly known as Bonnie Prince Charlie or the 'Young Pretender', had been born in exile in Rome. Intent on regaining his birthright, in 1745 with the promise of French assistance the Prince set sail for Scotland and raised his standard at Glenfinnan. His charm won over the Highland chiefs and (although support from France never materialized) he moved south, gathering about him a growing army that defeated all opposition. The force had reached Derby in early December 1745 when doubts began to set in: convinced that they could not take

59. Teapot and lid, *c. 1755*, depicting the Young
Pretender dressed as a Highland warrior and wearing
the Garter sash. This representation is based on a
medal issued in 1749. The lid is a replacement.

60. Portrait plaque of Prince Henry Benedict, glass
paste, after a medal produced in Rome by Otto
Hameram. The motto (The next after him) refers to
Henry Benedict's position in the succession following
his brother, Prince Charles Edward

London, his commanders persuaded the Prince
that they should return to Scotland. The pendu-
lum now swung in favour of King George's
troops, who harried the Highlanders northwards
(despite holding actions at Clifton and at Falkirk)
until they reached Culloden near Inverness,
where on 16 April 1746 they were totally crushed
by numerically superior, better-equipped and
better-disciplined regular forces under the Duke
of Cumberland.

Prince Charles escaped from the battlefield
and for months, with a price of £30,000 on his
head, he wandered through the Western
Highlands and Islands. Despite the risk of the
harshest punishments, he was never betrayed by
the Highland Scots and indeed one of the more
uplifting stories of that time is the tale told of
how Flora MacDonald of South Uist assisted
Prince Charles to evade capture by disguising
him as her Irish maidservant. In September 1746
he made his escape to the Continent, where he
was to die forty-two years later in Rome.

Prince Henry Benedict (1725–1807), the younger
brother of Charles Edward, was altogether a less
flamboyant character, resembling more the retir-
ing nature of his father. In 1747 he was created a
Cardinal and entered the Roman Catholic priest-
hood, ending any possibility that he might one
day be a claimant to the throne of England
(although, when his brother died, Prince Henry
styled himself Henry IX). During the
Napoleonic War, when his palace was sacked by
the French, the British government came to his
aid and George III gave him a small pension.
When he died, Henry left to the Prince Regent,
the future George IV, the few British crown
jewels still in his possession as well as the Sobieski
family jewels and the Stuart archives, so bringing
about a late reconciliation between the royal
houses of Stuart and Hanover. Henry was buried
in St. Peter's at Rome, along with his father and
his brother. Above their tomb was placed a handsome marble monument by Canova, commis-
sioned by the Prince Regent.

61. Flora MacDonald (1722–1790), by Alan Ramsay. She was persuaded to help Bonnie Prince Charlie escape his English pursuers as she sailed to Skye from South Uist. Flora was later to find herself celebrated as a romantic heroine, even though imprisoned in the Tower of London. It was while she was in London that Alan Ramsay painted her portrait.